Hello Kitty® Stationery Activity Book

by Kris Hirschmann

Scholastic Inc.

New York Toronto London Auckland Sydney
Mexico City New Delhi Hong Kong Buenos Aires

Illustrations by Yancey C. Labat
Photography by Rocco Melillo

ISBN 0-439-32837-3

12 11 10 9 8 7 6 5 4 3 2 1   1 2 3 4 5 6/0

Printed in the U.S.A.
First Scholastic printing, November 2001

Table of Contents

Sending Letters Is Fun!

Hello Kitty just loves getting letters from her friends. Don't you? Getting mail always makes Hello Kitty feel special. Hello Kitty likes to send letters to her friends, too, because she likes making her friends happy! It doesn't matter whether the letters are long or short. Any letter shows your friends that you're thinking about them.

Sometimes it's fun to make your letters extra special by adding drawings, cutouts, or other surprises. In this book, Hello Kitty shares with you nineteen of her most favorite stationery projects. Plus, she sends you love and kisses.

XXO

Hello Kitty

1

Let's Get Started

With this book you get twenty sheets of stationery and twenty envelopes, plus an ink pad and stamp set.

There are also some shapes printed on the next three pages of this book. You can trace these shapes to do some of the crafts or use them as examples to draw your own.

Everything else you need for these crafts can be found around your house. When you run out of stationery, you can make some more by cutting white or colored sheets of paper in half lengthwise.

To Trace a Shape:

Get some thin white paper that is easy to see through. (This is called white tracing paper in the instructions.) Place the paper on the shape you want to trace and draw all the lines. When you're done, you'll have a handmade copy of the shape!

Lightweight Cardboard:

Some of the crafts in this book call for lightweight cardboard. A manila file folder is perfect for this. So is an empty cereal box or thin craft board.

Shapes to Trace

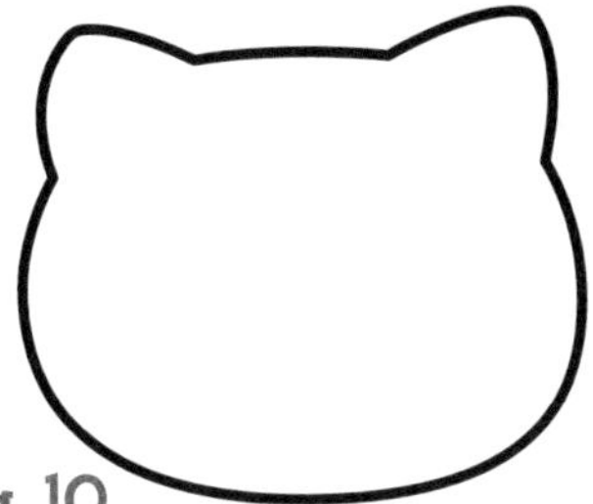

Pg. 10

Pg. 6

Pg. 8

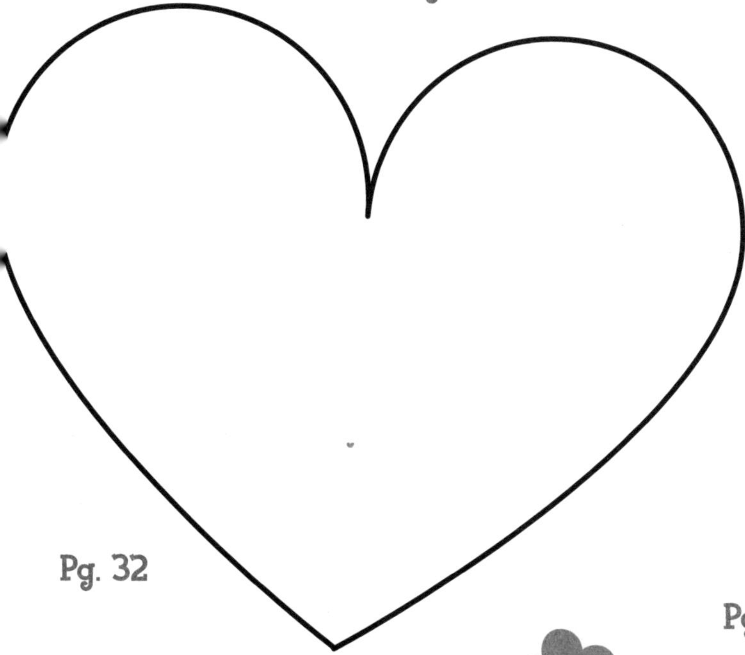

Pg. 32

Pg. 12

3

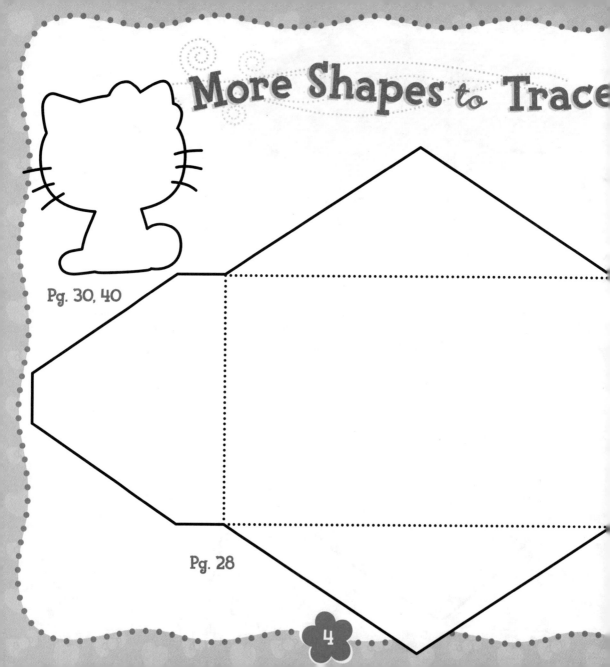

More Shapes to Trace

Pg. 30, 40

Pg. 28

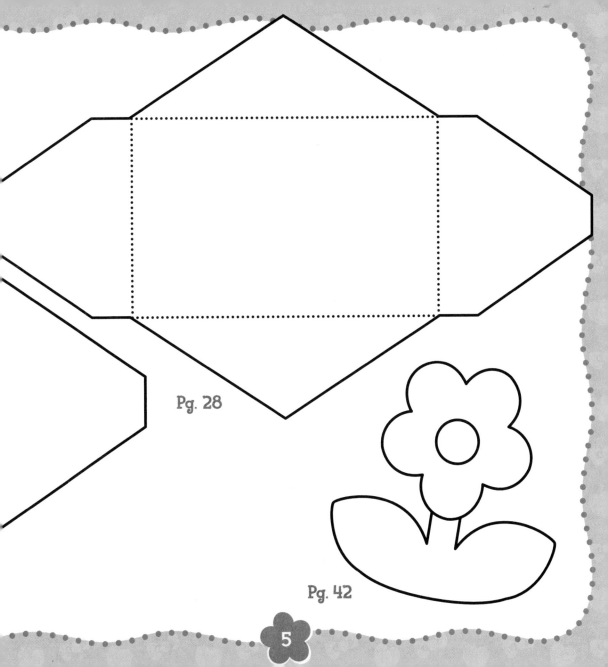

Pg. 28

Pg. 42

Cool Cutouts

The fun cutouts in this section are a perfect way
to show your friends you think they're special!

Heart Rainbow:

**Hearts say friendship! Make a pretty rainbow-colored heart border
on your stationery to show a friend how much you care.**

What You Do:

1. Trace the small
heart from
page 3 onto a
piece of white
tracing paper.
Cut it out.

2. Lay the heart cutout in the
upper left-hand corner of
a sheet of stationery, as
shown. Use any color pencil
to trace around the edges
of the cutout.

3. Move the cutout
next to the heart
you just traced
and trace around
the cutout again.

4. Repeat steps 2 and 3 five more times. When you're done, there will be seven hearts lined up.

5. Color the hearts in this order: red, orange, yellow, green, blue, violet, and indigo. That's all the colors of the rainbow!

6. Cut along the outer edges of the hearts as shown in the picture. When you're done, your stationery will have a really cool border.

Hello Kitty says:
Rainbows and hearts are two of the coolest things. Your heart rainbow is so pretty!

What You Need:

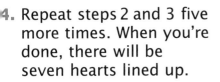

- White tracing paper
- Pencil
- Scissors
- One sheet of stationery
- Colored pencils

Hello Kitty in Your Pocket:

Make this adorable Hello Kitty and attach it to the top of a letter you are sending to a friend. When your friend is finished reading the letter, she can clip Hello Kitty to a pocket and take her everywhere!

What You Do:

1. Using a black pencil, trace the angel Hello Kitty from page 3 onto a piece of the tracing paper.

2. Draw and color Hello Kitty's dress, bow, and nose using colored pencils.

3. Use a glue stick to paste Hello Kitty to a piece of lightweight cardboard.

4. Cut around the edges of your Hello Kitty angel. Don't get too close to the lines or you might cut off Hello Kitty's whiskers!

5. Bend the inner part of a paper clip up a little bit. Use plenty of white glue to attach the larger part of the paper clip to the back of your angel Kitty.

6. Let the glue dry completely. This might take a couple of hours, so be patient. When the glue is dry, your guardian angel Hello Kitty is ready to travel!

Hello Kitty says:

Good friends take care of each other. Carry me with you and I'll be your good friend, too!

What You Need:

- White tracing paper
- Black pencil
- Colored pencils
- Glue stick
- Lightweight cardboard
- Scissors
- Paper clip
- White glue

Rubbing Fun

Hello Kitty thinks rubbings are neat! This technique lets you put textured or raised images onto flat paper. It's almost as good as making a copy, but you get to do all the work—and have all the fun, too!

Kitty Prints:

This letter is extra-fun to receive because it's covered with cute Hello Kitty heads!

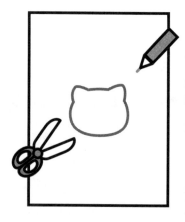

What You Do:

1. Trace the small Hello Kitty head from page 3 onto a piece of white tracing paper. Cut it out.

2. Set the stationery sheet on top of the cutout.

3. Rub the tip of a colored pencil back and forth over the cutout. A picture of Hello Kitty will appear!

4. Keep rubbing until Hello Kitty's whole head shows.

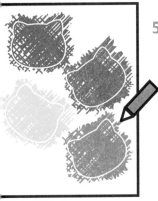

5. Repeat steps 2 through 4 as many times as you like, moving the cutout each time. You can tilt Hello Kitty's head any way you like before you rub!

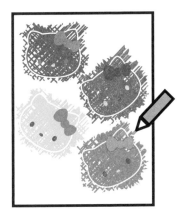

6. Use your colored pencils to give each kitty print two eyes, a nose, and a pretty bow.

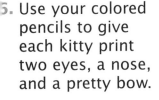

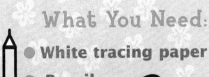

Hello Kitty **says:**

See how many Hello Kitty faces you can make on one sheet of stationery.

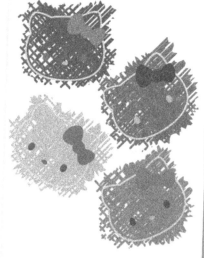

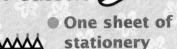

What You Need:

- White tracing paper
- Pencil
- Scissors
- One sheet of stationery
- Colored pencils

Bunny Love:

At first glance, your friend might not notice anything special about this stationery. But a closer look will reveal Hello Kitty's bunny friend, Kathy!

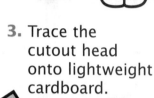

What You Do:

1. Trace Kathy's head from page 3 onto a piece of white tracing paper.

2. Cut it out.

3. Trace the cutout head onto lightweight cardboard.

4. Cut it out again.

5. Set a sheet of stationery on top of the cardboard cutout.

6. Erase around the edges of the cutout with a clean eraser. (Clean is important! A dirty eraser will smudge your stationery.) An imprint of Kathy's head will appear! (Be sure to hold the paper steady while you rub so that the paper doesn't wrinkle.)

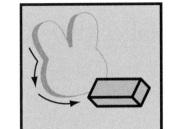

7. Repeat step 6 as many times as you like, moving the cutout each time.

Hello Kitty says:
You did this just for me? You're such a sweet friend!

What You Need:

- White tracing paper
- Pencil
- Scissors
- Lightweight cardboard
- One sheet of stationery
- Clean eraser

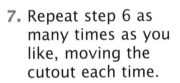

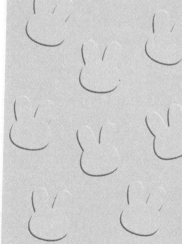

Yummy Hello Kitty Cookies:

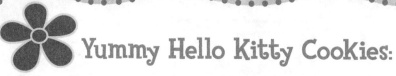

Does your friend have a sweet tooth?
If so, a dozen "cookies" will surely make her day!

What You Do:

1. Draw 12 circles on a brown paper bag. Each circle should be about 1 inch (2.5 cm) wide. Cut them out.

2. Decorate the circles like your favorite cookies!

For oatmeal-raisin cookies:
Lay a circle on a clean part of the sidewalk or a paved driveway. Rub the tip of a brown pencil back and forth over the circle to create a lumpy oatmeal-cookie texture. Then use a purple pencil to draw raisins.

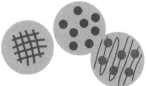

For chocolate-chip cookies:
Use a brown pencil to draw round chocolate chips.

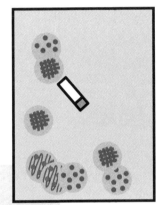

For peanut-butter cookies:
Use a brown pencil to draw crisscrosses.

3. Use a glue stick to paste the cookies to a sheet of stationery.

Hello Kitty says:
My twin sister, Mimmy, loves to bake cookies and share them with all our friends. Yummy!

What You Need:

- Brown paper bag
- Scissors
- Ruler
- Colored pencils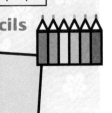
- Glue stick
- One sheet of stationery

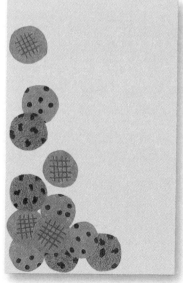

Stamp Stuff

There are two kinds of stamp activities in this section. One is the kind where you press ink shapes onto paper. The other is the kind that you stick onto envelopes. Hello Kitty thinks both kinds of stamps are a lot of fun, and hopefully you will, too!

 ## Fingerprint Pals:

No two people in the entire world have identical fingerprints. So this stationery is truly unique. Only you can make it!

What You Do:

1. Press any one of your fingers against your Hello Kitty ink pad.

2. Press your inky finger against a sheet of stationery. When you lift your finger, an ink print will remain!

3. Repeat steps 1 and 2 as many times as you like.

4. After the ink is dry, use a pen to draw arms, legs, faces, and hair on your fingerprint pals.

Hello Kitty
says:
You should make lots and lots of fingerprint pals. After all, you can never have too many friends!

What You Need:

- **Your Hello Kitty ink pad**
- **One sheet of stationery**
- **Pen**

Sponge Stamping:

This craft is super-easy to do, and the results are super-cool! Use a brand-new, clean sponge for the best results.

What You Do:

1. Cut any shape you like out of the sponge. (Make sure it's small enough so that you can fit it on the stationery several times.) You could make a heart, a flower, or even a butterfly.

2. Press the sponge shape against your Hello Kitty ink pad. Make sure you get it nice and inky.

3. Lightly press the inky shape against a sheet of your stationery to make a sponge print.

4. Repeat steps 2 and 3 as many times as you like. Be sure to let the ink dry completely— about five minutes.

Hello Kitty says:

Isn't it neat that an everyday sponge can make such pretty art?

What You Need:

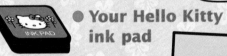

- Scissors
- Household sponge
- Your Hello Kitty ink pad
- One sheet of stationery

Special Delivery:

Letters that go through the mail need real stamps. But you can make pretend stamps for letters that will be hand-delivered!

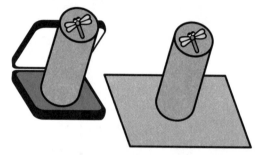

What You Do:

1. Press one of your rubber stamps against the stamp pad, then press it against a piece of colored paper to leave an ink picture.

2. Cut around the ink picture in a square or rectangle shape. You can cut wavy edges to make the shape look more like a real stamp.

3. Write some words on your "stamp" (you can write anything you want), and give your stamp a value.

4. Use a glue stick to paste your stamp to the upper right-hand corner of an envelope. Then hand-deliver your special letter to a friend!

Hello Kitty says:
It's so much fun to see me and my friends on your homemade special stamps!

What You Need:

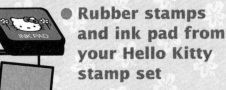

- Rubber stamps and ink pad from your Hello Kitty stamp set
- Colored paper
- Scissors
- Colored pencils
- Glue stick
- Envelope

I LOVE YOU

10¢

For Your Eyes Only

Sometimes Hello Kitty shares secrets when she's writing to her very closest friends, but she likes to keep her secrets private. Follow these crafts and you can send your friends some secret messages, too!

S.W.A.K:

S.W.A.K. means "sealed with a kiss." Make some fun kiss cutouts and use them to seal your envelope. Only your friend is allowed to break the seal!

What You Do:

1. Put a heavy coat of lipstick or lip gloss on your lips.

2. Kiss a piece of colored paper. You will leave behind a cute lip print.

3. Kiss the same piece of paper a few more times in different places, holding your lips in a slightly different position each time. (You might need to apply new lipstick in between each kiss to get a good print.) You can change lipstick colors if you want.

4. Cut out the very best lip prints.

5. Use a glue stick to paste the kiss cutouts over the sealed edge of an envelope.

Hello Kitty says:

You can draw "X's" near the lip prints. In letter writing, "X" stands for a Kiss!

What You Need:
- Lipstick or lip gloss
- Colored paper (lighter shades work best)
- Scissors
- Glue stick
- Finished letter in sealed envelope

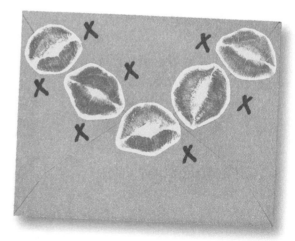

 Tiny Mail:

This neat folding trick helps you to make your letters very small before they are opened up. Little letters are easy to slip through locker vents or hide in backpacks. No one will notice them except you and your friend!

What You Do:

1. Fold the letter in half widthwise with the writing on the outside.

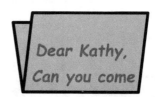

2. Fold down the front right-hand corner as shown, making sure the bottom edges are even.

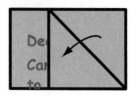

3. Fold down the front left-hand corner as shown, making sure the bottom edges are even.

4. Flip the letter over and repeat steps 2 and 3.

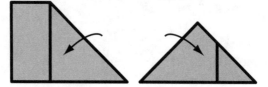

5. Open the letter along the middle fold. Set it on the table with the writing side facing up.

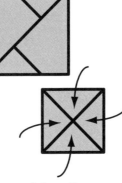

6. Fold in all four corners so that they meet in the middle.

7. Fold in all four corners again and seal with a sticker.

8. Write your friend's name on the other side of the folded letter. Your tiny mail is ready to be delivered!

Kathy

What You Need:

- **Finished one-page letter on your Hello Kitty stationery**

Dear Kathy,
Can you come to my house after dance class today?
Hello Kitty

- **Sticker**

Secret Message:

This looks like a regular letter. But there's a secret message hiding between the lines, and only you and your friend know how to make the secret message appear!

What You Do:

1. Use a colored pencil to write a message to your friend on a sheet of white stationery, leaving plenty of space between each line.

2. Use a white crayon or candle to write a secret message between the lines.

Dear Jeannie,

This letter is not quite what it appears to be. Call me and I'll tell you a great trick to reveal the hidden message. Remember it's for your eyes only!

Sara

Dear Jeannie,

This letter is not quite what it appears to be. Call me and I'll tell you a great trick to reveal the hidden message. Remember it's for your eyes only!

Sara

3. Give the secret letter to your friend!

Dear Jeannie,

This letter is not quite what it appears to be. Call me and I'll tell you a great trick to

reveal the hidden message. Remember own, but it's easy it's for your eyes only if you cover it with watercolor paint!

It is very hard to read on its

Sara

4. Tell your friend to brush the letter with watercolor paint. When she does, your secret message will appear!

Hello Kitty
says:
Shhh! Remember, good friends never tell each other's secrets!

What You Need:
- **Colored pencil**
- **One sheet of white stationery**
- **White crayon or birthday candle**

What Your Friend Needs:
- **Watercolor paint**
- **Paintbrush**

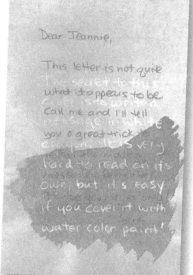

Dear Jeannie,

This letter is not quite what it appears to be. Call me and I'll tell you a great trick

It is very hard to read on its own, but it's easy if you cover it with water color paint!

Nesting Envelopes:

This message is so secret that your friend has to open three envelopes to get to it!

What You Do:

1. Trace the large envelope shape on page 4 onto a piece of white tracing paper. Cut it out.

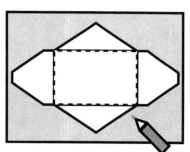

2. Lay the cutout on a piece of colored paper. Use a pencil to trace around the edges of the cutout. Then cut out the envelope.

3. Repeat steps 1 and 2 using the smaller envelope shape on page 5. For the prettiest results, use a different color paper the second time you repeat step 2.

4. Set the large envelope cutout on the table.

5. Fold in the side flaps as shown (along the dotted lines of the envelope shape).

6. Use a glue stick to spread a line of paste onto the bottom edges of the flaps you just folded.

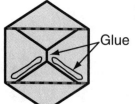

Glue

7. Fold up the bottom flap as shown (along the dotted line). Press along the edges to glue. You now have an envelope.

8. Repeat steps 4 through 7 using the small envelope cutout.

9. Cut out a piece of colored paper small enough to fit into the small envelope. Write a note on the paper and put it into the small envelope.

10. Fold down the top flap of the small envelope along the dotted line. Use the glue stick to seal the envelope, then put it into the large envelope.

11. Fold and seal the top flap of the new envelope, then put it into one of the envelopes that came in your kit.

12. Seal the last envelope by licking it. Your message should be safe within so many layers!

Hello Kitty says:

It's fun to open all those envelopes. You can't wait to read the letter!

What You Need:

- White tracing paper
- Pencil
- Scissors
- Colored paper
- Glue stick
- Envelope from this kit

Pop-up Cards

Making pop-up cards is a fun way to say hello to friends. It just takes a little bit of extra time. Some of these cards have some tricky folds, too. But the effort is worth it. Just imagine the look on your friend's face when she opens one of these fun notes!

From Kitty with Love:

A special friend pops up from this cool card to say "Hello!" You can write on the inside or the outside. It's up to you!

What You Do:

1. Fold a sheet of white stationery in half widthwise.

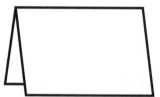

2. Open the sheet and place it on the picture of Hello Kitty on page 4. Position the paper so that Hello Kitty is in the middle, with her head above the fold and her body below the fold.

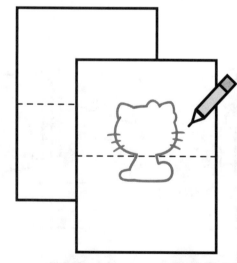

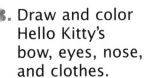

3. Draw and color Hello Kitty's bow, eyes, nose, and clothes.

4. Carefully cut around Hello Kitty's head. (Be careful—you don't want to trim her whiskers!) Don't cut below the fold line.

5. Fold the top of the stationery down, but leave Hello Kitty's head up.

6. Set the card on a table as shown. It's a note from Hello Kitty!

Hello Kitty says:
This is fun! I like popping up from your letter!

What You Need:

● **One sheet of stationery**
● **Colored pencils**
● **Scissors**

Beating Heart:

When you open this card and wiggle the edges, the pop-up heart inside looks like it's beating!

What You Do:

1. Trace the big heart from page 3 onto a piece of white tracing paper.

2. Cut it out.

3. Set the cutout heart on a piece of colored paper. Trace around the edges.

4. Cut out the colored heart.

5. Fold the colored heart in half.

6. Cut out two tabs from a piece of colored paper. (Each tab should be about the size of the rectangle at right—¾ high x 1¼ wide.) Fold both tabs in half.

7. Use a glue stick to paste the tabs to the back of the heart as shown.

8. Fold a piece of stationery in half, then open it back up. Position the heart and the card so their centerfolds line up. Let the heart pop up above the card just a little bit.

9. Use a glue stick to paste the loose half of each tab to the card.

10. When you close the card, fold the heart forward like this:

11. Open the card and watch the heart pop out. Wiggle the edges to make the heart beat!

Hello Kitty says:
Getting a card from a friend always makes my heart go pitter-patter!

What You Need:

- White tracing paper
- Pencil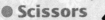
- Scissors
- Colored paper
- One sheet of stationery
- Glue stick

Singing Bird:

A cheerful bird pops out of this card to sing your friend a little song!

What You Do:

1. Set your circular object on a piece of colored paper. Trace around the edges.

2. Cut out the circle, then fold it in half. Cut about a 1 inch slit as shown.

3. Fold back the edges of the slit as shown. This will form 2 small triangles. Run your fingernail along the creases to make them nice and sharp.

4. Bend the triangles back up and open the circle. Lay it on a table.

5. Pinch along the creases so the paper pokes forward. Look at the picture of the finished craft on page 35 to see how it should look.

6. Draw two beady eyes on the circle. It's a bird with an open beak!

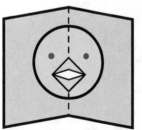

7. Fold a sheet of stationery in half, then open it back up. Position the bird and the card so their centerfolds line up.

8. Use a glue stick to paste the bird to the card. Be careful not to get any glue within the beak area.

9. When you close the card, fold the beak forward. You can see how this works in the picture of the finished craft at the bottom of this page.

10. Open the card. Wiggle the edges to see the bird sing!

Hello Kitty says:

Don't you love music? Chirp, chirp!

What You Need:

- Soup can or similar-size circular object
- Colored paper
- Colored pencils
- Scissors
- One sheet of stationery
- Glue stick

Message in a Flower:

This craft is a pop-up card and a secret message all in one!

What You Do:

1. Set your circular object on a sheet of colored paper. Trace around the edges.

2. Cut out the circle, then fold it in half.

3. Fold it in half again.

4. Lay the folded circle on a table. Lift one flap so it stands straight up.

5. Stick your finger into the flap. Press down until the flap flattens into a triangle shape. Run your fingernail along the edges to crease them.

6. Flip the paper over and lift the other flap so it stands straight up.

7. Repeat step 5.

8. Lift the shape and bend the flaps until they make a flower shape like this:

9. Fold a piece of stationery in half widthwise, then open it back up. Position the flower and the card so their centerfolds line up.

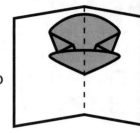

10. Use a glue stick to paste the edges of the flower to the card as shown.

11. Draw a stem and leaves below the flower if you want.

12. Open up the flower and write a secret message to your friend. Then push the flower back together. Close the card.

13. Open the card. The flower pops out—and it's a surprise for your friend!

Hello Kitty
says:

Flowers are always sweet, but a flower with a secret note is the sweetest of all!

What You Need:

- Tuna can or similar-size circular object
- Colored paper
- Colored pencils
- Scissors
- One sheet of stationery
- Glue stick

Surprise!

Hello Kitty loves surprises. This section has three neat "Surprise!" crafts that you can make for your pals.

Hidden Friends:

When you send a letter written on this stationery, you're also sending a bunch of secret friends! Just open the windows and they'll pop out to say "hi!"

What You Do:

1. Draw windows on one piece of stationery like this: Then cut along the lines you just drew. You can cut as many windows as you want, wherever you want.

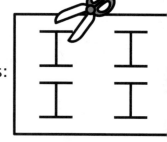

2. Open the windows wide. Then use a glue stick to spread paste on the back of the stationery. Be careful not to get any glue on the window flaps.

3. Set the glued paper onto a second sheet of stationery. Make sure to line up the edges. Press gently to stick the two pieces of paper together.

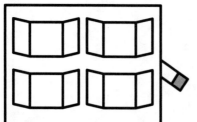

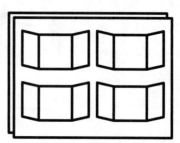

4. Put a sticker in each window or draw a small picture or write a tiny letter.

5. Close all the windows to hide the stickers, and send your letter off to your pal!

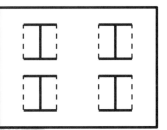

Hello Kitty **says:**

A friendly wave from an open window means "Hello!" in any language!

What You Need:

- Two sheets of stationery
- Ruler or other straight-edge
- Pencil
  - Scissors
  - Glue stick
- Your own stickers (optional)
- Colored pencils

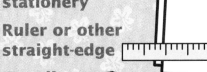

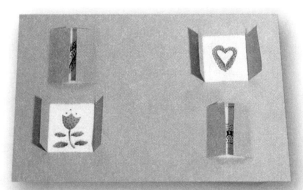

Hello Kitty's New Bow:

Hello Kitty loves to dress up. She especially likes new bows. Send a bow-changing Hello Kitty to your best friend!

What You Do:

1. Fold a sheet of white stationery in half widthwise.

2. Open the sheet and place it on the picture of Hello Kitty on page 4. Position the paper so that Hello Kitty is about ¼ inch (6 mm) below the fold.

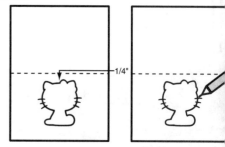

3. Using a black pencil, trace Hello Kitty onto the stationery sheet.

4. Draw and cut out Hello Kitty's bow. (The bow is little, so you have to be very careful. If you want, you could ask a grown-up to do it for you using a craft knife.)

5. Draw and color Hello Kitty's eyes, nose, and clothes.

6. Use a glue stick to spread paste on the stationery. Look at the picture to see where to put the paste.

7. Fold down the top flap (the one with Hello Kitty on it). Press gently to stick the flaps together.

8. Cut a long tab out of lightweight cardboard. The tab should measure about 1 x 6 inches (2.5 x 15 cm).

9. Color the tab as shown. Write "Pull" on the right-hand side.

Hello Kitty says:
You should always have lots of bows— so you can wear a different one every day!

10. Insert the tab into the unglued slot at the top right-hand corner of the card.

11. Pull the tab back and forth to change the color of Hello Kitty's bow!

What You Need:

- Tracing paper
- One sheet of white stationery
- Ruler
- Colored pencils
- Scissors
- Glue stick
- Lightweight cardboard

Friendship Flower:

This pretty flower is just like your special friendship. It's always growing!

What You Do:

1. Trace the flower from page 5 onto the center of a piece of white stationery.

2. Color the flower any way you like.

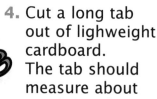

3. Use a glue stick to paste the flower to a piece of lightweight cardboard. Then cut around the edges.

4. Cut a long tab out of lighweight cardboard. The tab should measure about 1 x 6.5 inches (2.5 x 16.5 cm).

5. Bend up the bottom of the tab 1/2 inch (1.2 cm).

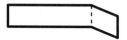

6. Fold up the bottom one-third of a stationery sheet. Use a glue stick to seal the outer edges as shown.

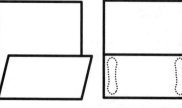

Glue

7. Cut two slits as shown. The slits should be just a little bit wider than the tab you made in step 4.

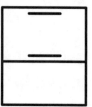

8. Insert the tab up through the slits as shown. Pull it up as far as it will go. Write "Pull" on the inside of the very top of the tab.

9. Use a glue stick to spread paste on the tab's bottom flap. Stick the flower to the flap as shown.

10. Push the flower down until it is hidden inside the folded part of the stationery.

11. Pull up on the tab to make the flower "grow"!

Hello Kitty says:

Wow, this was a hard activity! But you did such a good job!

What You Need:

- **Two pieces of white stationery**
- **Pencil**
- **Colored pencils**
- **Glue stick**
- **Lightweight cardboard**
- **Scissors**
- **Ruler**

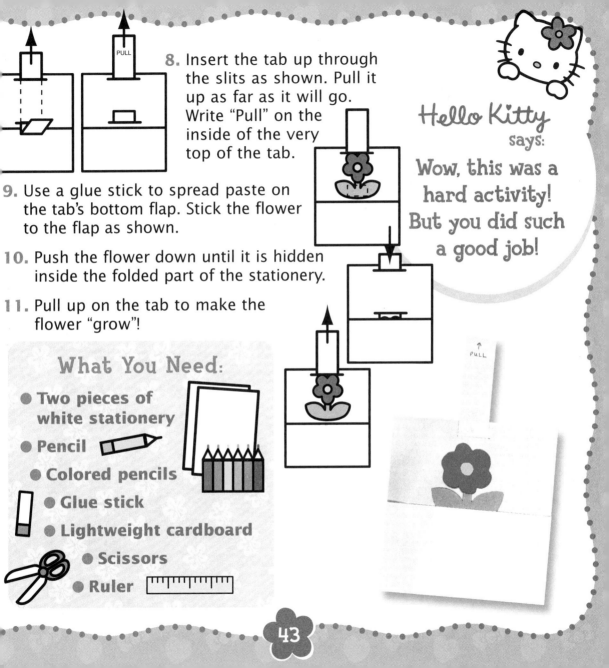

43

Hello Kitty Crafts Are Fun!

Hope you enjoyed all of Hello Kitty's favorite stationery activities. They're a lot of fun— and Hello Kitty is sure your friends will really like getting your special letters! But you don't have to stop just because you finished this book. You can keep going by making up your own projects. In fact, sometimes your own ideas are the best of all.

No matter what you create, have a great time!